Spinoza's Science:
The Ethics of Knowledge

Louis Russell

Dedication

Τοῖς ἀνιαροῖς καὶ νηπιοῖς, ἄνευ γὰρ τῆς ὧν ἀπείρου παραμυθίας, οὔποτε ἐγνώκοιμι ἄν τὸν Σπινόζαν.

CONTENTS

[This page is intentionally left blank]

INTRODUCTION

In his famous work, *Ethics Demonstrated in Geometric Order*, Baruch Spinoza invites the philosopher to explore the possibility of pure intellectual joy as a way of human life. This book serves as a philosophical introduction to the best of Spinoza's offerings in the *Ethics*: namely, how the performance of Spinozist science itself constitutes the acme of human achievement. In a short space, I shall trace Spinoza's trifold distinction between kinds of knowledge, then uncover the ethical conclusions one must necessarily draw should Spinoza's premises be taken as acceptable.

Having studied Spinoza for some time, I have at different moments confronted different aspects of the same dominant strain in his thinking: this line of force concerns the ethical implications of what we think we know, what we do know, and what we can know, if only we exercise our reason. This undercurrent in the *Ethics* does not simply tie knowledge to ethics but sets the grasping of a certain kind of knowledge—intuitive science—equal to the human being's highest ethical calling. But any confrontation with this line of thought outside the graduate seminar, outside the Latin language, outside of Spinoza's basic premise for his normative prescriptions—the pursuit of an active, constant joy that arises necessarily from a rational engagement with lived experience—hazards to yield more of the confusion and frustration that Spinoza labored to cure than that persistent joy he labored to inculcate in his readers. The purpose of this book is to condense this dominant strain of his thinking in a way that will assist with either an academic or a personal reading of the *Ethics*, an aim which will conceptually focus the reader's attention on the proverbial forest, as well as its most beautiful trees.

This is largely a book about knowledge, or how Spinoza marries knowing with being, and further how he thinks of being as the foundation of ethics. In order to present a clear and contrastive account of how Spinoza conceives of knowledge (*cognitio*), we must first understand how things go wrong for us knowers. This going wrong, Spinoza calls 'the first kind of knowledge'. Yet, like the *Ethics* itself, statements about the strengths of Spinozism will require a preliminary backdrop that fills Spinoza's key concepts in with content. Before speaking about Spinoza's epistemological theses, I must begin with a discussion of his method and its place in the history of philosophy.

SPINOZA'S METHOD

Spinoza in his own way summons the reader to live a certain strain of the life examined. His three-tiered epistemology represents different degrees of philosophical reflection, soundness, and knowledge. The charge 'not to believe everything you hear' and to discern carefully the true from the false is not new. Nor is it beyond the common understanding of what an average person, who has read little or no philosophy will in some way discover on their own.[1] But, for Spinoza, the invocation of the intellect necessarily involves performative degrees of actualization. In the next section I consider the first kind of knowledge, the initial and shallowest grade of human knowing when taken as the thing in itself. Before I set forth a reading of Spinoza's epistemological views, it will serve the reader well to grasp more concerning the unstated assumptions that come along with the manner and style—the *method*—in which Spinoza wrote his *opus*. My purpose is neither to insert a tome into the canon of literature on Spinoza's method, nor even an article into the academic literature, but rather to offer briefly the simple aspects of it my reader needs in order to continue toward Spinoza's epistemology.[2]

Anyone who opens a copy of the *Ethics* will immediately notice the geometric form in which Spinoza elects to mount his arguments. He styles the text after the formal Euclidean proofs of geometric properties, but what this mode of argumentation is and a clear determination as to why Spinoza chose it generally produces controversy among interpreters. Academic controversy has its rightful place, and that place is not

---

[1] Yet, there is a difference between knowing by accident and knowing by logical necessity.

[2] For such a tome, see Garrett (2011).

within these pages. My purpose will not be to conduct the wide-ranging investigation of historical figures like Thomas Hobbes, Giacomo Zabarella, and René Descartes that would allow for a technical and esoteric reading of Spinozist metaphysical geometry. I aim to simplify the problem for my reader rather than to stultify the possibility of taking anything from the later portions of the work due to an excess of data. In brief, I shall select the most plausible interpretations and present them here. But it is important to flag the controversy so that the reader sees the text philosophically, approaches it with more questions than prejudices.

The simplest explanation as to why Spinoza took up the geometric style of argumentation is that he appropriated the Cartesian[3] distinction between analytic and synthetic methods. Unfortunately, Descartes never formally defines either approach. Spinoza certainly contested elements of this methodical distinction, but the general clue as to how to structure his own treatise arose from the way in which Descartes interpreted and appropriated the basic vocabulary of Aristotelian epistemology and method. The geometric style essentially corresponds to synthesis, but most scholars today would agree that Spinoza wrote the *Ethics* in a way that made use

---

[3] I call the analytic-synthetic distinction 'Cartesian', but when studying the history of philosophy, it is generally wise advisable to keep the history of philosophy in mind. Here, Descartes simply reads Aristotle aloud. Both the basic distinction itself and its application to specific subject matter originate in Aristotle. For Aristotle, analysis involves the mental activity the ranges from coming to know what a thing is to the full-bodied experience of coming to know the why of its being; synthesis involves taking a subject (the existence of which you have analytically confirmed) and saying something—anything— about it. The fancy word for saying something about a subject is 'predication', the Latinization of the Greek word for 'category' *katégoria*. For Aristotle, we can categorize the things we encounter once we know them analytically. Descartes either took this straight from Aristotle or from Aristotelian Scholastics. See *Posterior Analytics B.19 and Nicomachean Ethics A.7, 1098a26-1098b9*.

of both methodical forms. Before I turn to Spinoza's method, I must briefly summarize Descartes's interpretations of analysis and synthesis in turn in order to give context to the problem of how Spinoza both inherited and challenged Descartes's permutation of Aristotelian philosophy and rhetoric.

Descartes seldom offers insight into the meaning of analysis and synthesis, and where he speaks directly of either, he does so sparsely. But he does tell us that his *Meditations* are exclusively analytic. For him, analysis reveals the true means by which a thing was discovered 'methodically and as it were *a priori*'.[4] Famously, the *a priori* truth in Descartes's *Meditations*, the Archimedean point which serves as the basis of his clear and distinct perceptions, is that he thinks. This 'I think' is known as the *cogito*. The *cogito* is an analytic truth, because the fact that he thinks comes prior to the possibility of doubting that he thinks. But Descartes does not structure his *Meditations* by baldly asserting that he thinks and therefore is. Instead, he takes the reader through the precise process of his own thoughts so as to create again his own experience in the person who follows him carefully. The analytic method seems easily explained as a metaphor for the way in which human beings actually develop the principles of their knowledge.

Synthesis, on the other hand, inverts the analytic method in that it begins by an assumption of the sorts of premises that the analytic method discovers. It is the *a posteriori* search for a conclusion that demonstrates the truth of that conclusion by means of definitions, axioms, postulates, propositions, demonstrations, etc. Best suited to geometry, as Descartes reports, Cartesian synthesis logically demonstrates the necessity of the conclusion

---

[4] René Descartes, *Selected Philosophical Writings*, trans. John Cottingham, Robert Stoothoff, and Dugald Murdoch (New York, NY: Cambridge University Press, 1998), 150-152.

step by step so as to persuade even the most stubborn. The trouble with the use of synthesis for the purpose of demonstrating metaphysical truths, says Descartes, is that such truths are not initially self-evident. If the philosopher simply puts them forward, they can easily be denied, despite that anyone who hears a discursive analysis thereof would accept them. Importantly, the philosopher takes as the premises of synthetic arguments those arguments at which he has arrived by the analytic method.

Descartes seems to have adapted the Aristotelian epistemological precept to fit philosophical style to the object of investigation, and further to have observed analysis and synthesis as modes of metaphysical rhetoric. Each serve as a way to persuade a certain kind of person of a certain kind of truth. For Descartes, the author need not merely adapt writing style to subject matter, but also writing style to the audience. And Spinoza explicitly inherited this rhetorical angle on philosophical writing, which he took up in his work *Principles of Cartesian Philosophy*, for the sake of instructing his childish but talented student Casearius. Cartesian Synthesis lays bare the logical bases for a conclusion in such a way that if one accepts the premises, the conclusion necessarily follows. As a result, it serves a certain set of pedagogical purposes, a didactic instrument that compels the reader according to the force of logic itself.

On my reading, Spinoza straightforwardly employs both techniques in the *Ethics*. I argue that the first two Parts of the *Ethics* contain the purest form of synthesis. The definitions at the beginning of the first two Parts mark Spinoza's synthetic intentions; he arrived at these definitions in analytic fashion. It is the prerogative of readers to come to understand these in their own way or through philosophical training. However, even in these two Parts of the text that contain the most rarified synthetic content, Spinoza includes in them lengthy scholia, written in analytic prose, that seem to serve analytic purposes.

While Spinoza clearly adheres to a synthetic structure in the beginning of the text, the last three Parts each include an introductory essay, in addition to scholia, that resembles Cartesian analysis. Doubtless, the reader of the *Ethics* does encounter a work intended to be read as a stylistic unity. But, at some point in the text, Spinoza or the text's editors adopted analytic procedures for persuading the reader of the metaphysical and ethical premises that initiate the reader into the basic argument. In order to have any hope of persuading the reader, Spinoza had to offer access to the analytic thought processes behind what would otherwise seem like truisms or even haphazard assumptions. The dominant method is synthetic, but, especially in the latter three Parts, when Spinoza relies increasingly on his own experience and his own way of life, he elects to offer the reader (and perhaps himself) a justification as to why one should accept the premises.

What is true, I think, is that Spinoza grew epistemologically fatigued toward the later stages of the work. The dogmatic confidence in his metaphysical theories that allowed for clean synthesis in the beginning of the work waned as the material became increasingly reliant on his own experiences. More and more, Spinoza came to rely on hypotheses in which he did not have the same level of confidence. Edwin Curley observes this as well, though phrases it differently.[5] Spinoza's lengthy explanations of his ethical precepts exemplify the merit of the roughly put thesis that, in general, the work gets progressively less synthetic as it continues. Especially in

---

[5] Edwin M. Curley, "Experience in Spinoza's Theory of Knowledge," ed. Marjorie Grene, in *Spinoza: A Collection of Critical Essays* (Garden City, NY: Anchor Press/Doubleday, 1973), 58.

Parts IV and V, he was not so much deducing the consequences of analytic truths for his reader, but actually inventing them as he went along. That is not to say that what he discovered is useless. Nor is there anything wrong with inventing. My point is that the writing in later Parts arrives in the same synthetic dress as the earlier, but the subject matter really is analytic. Spinoza maintained the synthetic style, because he had committed himself to a geometric *opus*. But formally synthetic does not necessarily imply substantially synthetic. He simply kept laying out his propositions in geometric style, because after all, he had promised, at least to himself, an *Ethics Demonstrated in Geometric Order*. This ambivalence between the synthetic form of the text itself and the waning certainty that Spinoza shows in the later precepts that he determines implies that the reader must reader carefully parse how Spinoza signifies or qualifies his own epistemic position toward the particular statement. I must emphasize that there is no simple way to read the text: the more fruitful and genuinely philosophical interpretive stance accounts for the dual possibility that Spinoza's statements, especially in parts IV and V, are perhaps both analytic and synthetic in various ways.

The problem that I have just been tracing concerns the extent to which Spinoza believes that his ethical claims apply to all human beings *qua* human. The last three Parts of the *Ethics* involve such strong theses that, if they were written in true synthetic form and as logical demonstrations, then they would offer regulatory principles on how all people ought to behave. I shall explore in this book the side of the debate that Spinoza in general believes that he is unlocking the ethical principles to which all people ought to adhere. There is textual merit to this view; and it certainly adds rhetorical force—perhaps in excess—to his ethical claims.

Spinoza's synthetic layout allows him to accelerate into the latter stages of the text despite his misgivings that he will be able to prescribe a single way of being (and proscribe others) for the sum of human kind. this acceleration into the more challenging ethical precepts *as synthetic truths* renders his philosophy radical because it entails a) that he believes he has logically proven his propositions to be true and b) that he has labored sufficiently to analyze the premises that govern his conclusions. This radicality, though there are notable and important exceptions to it, is the abominable fruit of his work. But there is little doubt that Spinoza's selection of the geometric method wants to incorporate into everyday ethics that same predictive power of science and mathematics for the sake of a complete roadmap for those who grasp the basic analytic truths on which the text is founded. Such a 'complete roadmap for life' is often called a 'religion'. But certainly, he does not want to impose a religion upon his readers.

Recall that Descartes's *Meditations* are intended to offer a justification of theology that has its basis in natural science. Now, if the Copernican revolution has proven that the natural sciences dictate the laws of the universe to religion, and not the other way around, then one can likewise infer that the ethical principles that undergird religion are just as open to criticism. In what way can I determine that the ethical teachings one finds in monotheistic religions have a sound logical basis? If anyone who is not a member of such a religion would listen to its ethical precepts, then one must offer a justification for those precepts that does not rely on the God of a certain faith alone as a justificatory principle. Spinoza offers a rationalist account of why one might undertake an ethical life *without* any need for an organized religion as a means of persuasion. But Spinoza's commitment to a form of monotheism similar to monotheistic conceptions of God leads him to believe that perhaps ethics can be a science just like science is. On the postmodern view, this is an absurd idea. In order to depict the precise radicality of Spinoza's view and its implications, I shall use contrast: let's briefly consider the Aristotelian account of knowledge, and particularly Aristotle's distinction between the kind of thing that must be so and the kind of thing that can be otherwise.

For Aristotle, there is an inherent distinction between two kinds of objects of human knowledge. The first of the two involve things that are necessarily true— i.e., they *could not be otherwise*. In this class, we find the scientific knowledge that Aristotle calls *epistêmê*. These truths are demonstrable in syllogistic form. A fact about which we have apodictic certainty—that we know scientifically—is of the sort that a) we derived it according to the rules of logical validity b) we have sufficient experience with the kind of thing in question that we can be *certain* that our premises are true. The example you may have heard in Logic 101 goes as follows:

1.   All men are mortal.
2.   Socrates is a man.
3.   Therefore, Socrates is mortal.

I call this argument logically valid because, if the premises are true, then the conclusion (3) must follow. Suspending skeptical and philosophical concerns about the nature of 'being mortal' or 'being human' and the larger question about the contexts in which these things are said to be 'real', I would also assert that the premises (1) and (2) are true. The process of inferring the conclusion from the first two premises is what Aristotle calls *apodeixis* or demonstration. For Aristotle, I can know that all men are mortal, because I have sufficient experience with human kind to know that, as Homer puts it, 'Human generations are like leaves in their seasons.'[6] In addition, I have a clear and unproblematic picture of what a human being is and

---

[6] Trans. Lombardo, 116.

am able to identify things in the world that are 'human'. Because I can identify Socrates as the kind of thing one calls human, and because I know from a lengthy series of generally reliable experiences that all human beings have the property of being mortal, I can know with apodictic certainty that Socrates is mortal. Aristotle founds his approach to science on this form of reasoning: scientists collect basic premises that they find incontrovertible or at least worthy of being treated as such, and then they perform logical operations on the basis of the experiential principles that serve as their premises. What makes the conclusion scientific knowledge (or in Greek *epistêmê*) is that the proposition *must* be true. And Socrates always and in every case involves the property of being mortal. This knowledge, for Aristotle, is scientific (*epistêmonikon*) and incontrovertible.

But there is another basic form of knowledge called *craft knowledge* (*technê*). And this kind of knowledge entails objects of knowledge whose properties *can be otherwise*. I might take an example of this sort of proposition to be, Aristotle is sitting. This indicative statement could certainly be true, but it is only true in certain cases. If Aristotle is standing, then the proposition is false. The subject Aristotle does not always and in every case involve the property of 'being seated'. So, this form of knowledge is about things that require attention to context. Propositions of this sort are sometimes true and sometimes false, and this is so owing to the complexity of the situations in which people apply them. The person who possesses *craft knowledge* knows how to produce the sort of end result or product, oftentimes a practical one, that requires situational attention.

I shall now briefly take Aristotle's example of bravery as a way to demonstrate what this means. Aristotle calls the emotional state that underlies bravery 'confidence'; its inverse is fear. Initially, the word confidence sounds unequivocally good and fear unequivocally bad. But Aristotle warns us that confidence is only good in relation to certain situations. Criminals who are confident that they can get away with a crime would actually benefit more from the fear of punishment than from confidence. Criminal confidence here is not bravery, but rashness. On the other hand, a battalion of soldiers who bravely thwart an enemy attack may be afraid, may not at all be confident in their ability to survive, but would do so rightly if, for instance, they could not escape without being killed anyway. For Aristotle, certain virtues call for attention to the situation. When situational attention is called for, the propositional object of knowledge could be otherwise. Their truth or falsity depends on the occasion in which one applies them. All right: now that the reader is heartily equipped with the distinction between the necessary and things that can be otherwise, I shall return to Spinoza's radical departure from this intuitive Aristotelian precept.

There are two ways of reading Spinoza's application of the geometric method toward the more experientially based stages of the *Ethics*: either it is a beautiful error or no error at all. Knowing the nuances of the Aristotelian position, I struggled at first to appreciate how Spinoza could possibly attempt to offer a unified prescription for how I ought to feel and ought to behave in every single possible situation. Surely, this form of knowledge must be related to the situation I'm in. And if it's always related to the situation I'm in, then one proposition simply won't do. Such a proposition would be endlessly fallible. At a glance, his attempt to normalize one intellectual state emotion and to outlaw others renders his philosophy vulnerable to severe criticism. This daring move, however, is precisely what ought to dazzle the reader.

In applying geometric synthesis to the latter stages of the *Ethics*, regions of the text that deal with issues of the emotional normativity that one would think require attention to the situation, Spinoza implies that he accepts that a geometry of metaphysical ethics is possible. Leave off for the moment the problem of whether or not he actually accomplishes this. The philosopher can, Spinoza thinks, derive ethical truths about emotions and about ethical practice that hold sway over *every possible human action*. Put in another way—one way of being effects the highest human happiness in every possible situation.

Now, I have argued that Spinoza rather boldly stuck with formal synthesis in the latter stages of the *Ethics*, despite his evident doubt in the project's feasibility. This is certainly so. But his analytic wavering does not imply that the possibility of uncovering necessary ethical truths about human psychology did not entice him to select the synthetic method to begin with. Though he is not the first to propose such a thesis, of the sort that we find in dogmatic religious texts, this almost unbelievably strong normativity yields a philosophically and ethically radical position, especially within the context of postmodern culture. In part accidentally, in part purposely, Spinoza's *Ethics* opens the door to the possibility of a science of ethical behavior that has the same predictive power as, e.g., mathematical physics. This science, for Spinoza, becomes radically available in proportion to how well we understand discernible truths concerning the complex workings of the human body.

To sum up, the basic question is whether or not it is possible to prescribe a single ethical disposition that regulates how all human beings ought to behave toward the word at all times. Spinoza's selection of the geometric method even for the more experiential phases of his text reveals that Spinoza thought (or at least persuaded himself into outwardly believing) that, Yes, there is a correct answer to the problem. In other words, there is a way of being that singly solves the problem of how to behave amidst the various difficulties of human life.

Whether or not Spinoza accurately depicts that way of being is one question, but his attempt to demonstrate his view geometrically and naturalistically is nothing short of radical, especially in light of the long history of practical Aristotelianism, a view that urges attention to situational saliences. Having now detailed the contrast between the Aristotelian and the Spinozist accounts of the possibilities for ethical norms, I shall now turn to Spinoza's three kinds of knowledge.

RANDOM EXPERIENCE

T he title of this section, random experience (*experientia vaga*), derives from what Spinoza thinks of as the basis for the first of three kinds of knowledge in the *Ethics*. It is clear to people with no training in philosophy whatsoever that one does not want their knowledge to be based on happenstance, but on necessity. Spinoza calls the first kind of knowledge opinion or imagination; in this mental state, the mind takes the local way things seem as the ultimate way things are. This basing of our knowledge on the way things seem randomizes what we think we know.

Any discussion of Spinozist epistemology will necessarily refer us to a particular part of the Ethics (IIP40S2), where he offers clear definitions of those three kinds. *Cognitio*, the Latin word often translated as 'knowledge', is a genus or a kind of state of the mind, and the three kinds of knowledge are subdivisions or species of that genus. Although English speakers today might think of genus and species as terms in biology, these terms have their origin in the Aristotelian philosophy and Scholasticism that used them as ways of categorizing and sub-categorizing the various kinds of furniture of the universe. Spinoza thinks that each kind of knowledge is rightly called knowledge, but that each kind primarily differs in the degree of precision and certitude by which one can judge each thought to be true or false.

The first kind of knowledge certainly does not rank first in precision and truth. Spinoza characterizes knowings of the first kind as confused, mutilated, and inadequate (IIP29C). And here, he refers us to the term perception, which for Spinoza entails a passive psychological event in the mind that arises not as a result of but as a direct instance of the impingement of external objects on our sensory organs. For Spinoza, who adheres to a doctrine called parallelism, which states that there is no distinction whatsoever between mind and body, but rather that they are really one no matter how we speak about them, our sensations essentially are our perceptions. When some external object affects our sensory organs, that object makes an impression in the mind. The mental impression is the perception of the object; and perception is passive because the mind does not necessarily do any work to interpret the true nature of that which acts upon it. Because the mind in this state unreflectively and unquestioningly receives information about the world, Spinoza thinks of this form of knowledge as the raw materials for deeper modes of understanding. And, because the contents of our sensory experience are merely raw materials, the intellect has not made any rational sense of them.

Not to have made rational sense of our experience means precisely that the person does not use their rational faculties in order to stabilize the way they approach the input but are at the whim of whatever information they receive. And the nature of being at the whim of random inputs leads a person to have ideas that may or may not stack up well next to what there actually is. Spinoza develops this picture by using the term 'confused', which derives from the Latin words *cum* (together) and *fundo* (I pour). Confusion, particularly in Latin, literally involves the mental state of mixing one thing up with another—a confused thought consists in the result of two or more jumbled thoughts that call for discursive thinking to separate them. In confusion, we fail to discern the difference between how the human body perceives a thing, i.e., how it acts on our sensory organs and how we interpret that impression, and that thing's essential properties. The task is to untie the way what we believe a thing to be from how a thing acts on our sensory organs and emotions.

For Spinoza, when an external thing leads to a perceptual state in the human mind, the most a person can know about the external thing on the basis of that state is that he is in it while he senses the external thing. If that sounds confusing, take it this way: no perceptual experience *alone* ever necessarily reveals the essential properties of the thing we perceive. What the percipient know and all that they know is that they are perceiving. The ability to untie these two facts—the way I perceive or think about a thing and the thing's true nature itself— is preliminarily key. Knowledge based on random experience lumps together all sensory and psychological experience of singular things with the thing itself. The first kind of knowledge counts *what the thing does to the mind* as *what the thing is*.

A common example is a person who sees a spider and becomes frightened. He might be tempted to accept a premise such as 'The spider has an innate property of scariness' rather than something like 'My body has a physiological stress response to the sight of the spider.' Now, one can sometimes unpack thoughts like 'The spider is scary' into something like the latter, but in the first kind of knowledge this does not happen. Childishly, mental states that Spinoza calls the first kind of knowledge takes 'scariness' as a sort of necessary property of the spider.

Spinoza is particularly concerned with the effect that human emotions have on the mind's ability to think rationally. A better example would be a couple who are having an argument at the kitchen counter. In the heat of the moment, Partner A says, *You aren't listening to me*. Partner B may simply not be answering because of this assumption: *This person's anger is making it impossible to have a productive conversation*. But perhaps Partner A is enthusiastic about solving the problem. In either case, each partner has made an inference on the basis his or her own perceptions of the other partner's behavior. There may or may not be good reasons for those inferences; the point is that anger or fear can affect the kind of thoughts that a person has in response to someone else.

Recall that Spinoza calls the first kind of knowledge 'opinion' or 'imagination'. The term opinion ought to call to mind the sociolinguistic background according to which people interpret their sensory experience. Perhaps a child who sees a spider and is frightened has taken cues from situation in which parents or others reacted to the sight of spiders with fear. Perhaps the thought came from a television show or some other place. The sociolinguistic background that allows us to take for granted that a spider is scary serves as a store of ideas that allows people to navigate the world they live in. But, when one fails to make proper use of reason, when one accepts this sociolinguistic background as a sort of 'given' that speaks for itself without the need for any evidential verification, then what Spinoza thinks of as 'opinion' holds that person in its sway. The concept of a spider's being scary is perhaps a trite example. So is the idea of the couple who talks at, around, and past one another. But the philosophical point is far from trivial.

If we up the ante to a much more serious context, like a legal proceeding, the importance of getting things right becomes clear. What validity would a law court have if it should judge the 'facts' of a case on the basis of emotion and perception alone? The 'ver' in 'verdict'—which comes from the Latin adjective *verus, vera, verum* and means 'true'—would be a dreadful irony, for a verdict would only 'truly' represent the legal team that best manipulated prejudices, emotions, and sensory organs of the jurors. A verdict would consist in nothing more than an annunciation of the way things *seem to a jury* rather than *the fact of the matter*.

Strangely, many cases are judged on the basis of spotty evidence, 'gut feelings'—just *knowing* it, and coerced confessions. The National Registry of

Exonerations counted 139 exonerations in 2017 alone. Those exonerations result from perjurious testimonies, false confessions, misidentifications, and other forms of official misconduct. But even in the social spaces where the stakes are the highest, as they are in court proceedings, specious evidence and gut feelings often suffice to persuade the juries that are tasked with executing justice to convict people who never committed those crimes. Spinoza calls the validity of these immediate perceptions into question; he thinks that people must reflect on the way things appear and on how emotions that arise because of those appearances influence the percipient's perspective of the truth in order to access a greater degree of certainty in regard to states of affairs in the world.

The first kind of knowledge involves, in short, the intellectual mistake of taking appearance as reality, what seems right actually to be true. When perceivers take appearance as reality, they not only potentially have the wrong answer, but they close the door on other ways things could possibly be interpreted. This is what Spinoza means by '*Omnis determinatio est negatio*' (every determination is negation). Appearance, for Spinoza, is part of reality, but not reality as such. When people take the simple impression they receive from a thing as the sole means for justifying how they think the thing actually is, their dedication to the wrong answer also entails also that, as long as they hold it, they can never have the correct one. All the rational agent knows on the basis of an appearance is that things appear a certain way. Blending together that things *appear* a certain way with their *being* a certain way involves the confused and mutilated ideas about the world that Spinoza attributes to the first kind of knowledge. Why the project of disconnecting the appearance of a thing or situation from the idea of its essence must not be taken lightly should now be a tad clearer, at least for anyone who thinks it paramount that anyone person held responsible for a crime has actually committed it.

COMMON NOTIONS

I n the previous chapter I demonstrated how Spinoza problematizes any episode of knowing that is based entirely on the perceptual knowledge that consist in a compound between sensations and emotions. Rather than leave knowledge up to random experience, Spinoza wants to depict axiomatic principles by which the mind can rationally discern truth from falsity. Following Descartes, he calls these axioms 'common notions'. I find unproblematic the following two theses: (1) these common notions correspond to certain kinds of conclusions reached in analytic reasoning; and (2) Spinoza intends us to read his axioms at the beginning of each Part as the common notions—taken together, these constitute reason itself. In what follows, I shall say more about the concept of common notions, then offer my view on how best to apply Spinoza's ideas.

As with the distinction between the analytic and synthetic methods, I said a moment ago that Spinoza appropriated the term 'common notions' from Descartes, who in fact borrowed the phrase (*koinai ennoiai*) from the Euclidean concept of geometric axioms. For Euclid, the common notions are self-evident and serve as the starting points for geometric deduction. But Descartes and Spinoza radicalize the geometric principles by appropriating the concept from the fields of pure mathematics to metaphysics or first philosophy. Having identified the need for a synthetic exposition of Cartesian metaphysics, Spinoza advances Descartes's work by axiomatically deducing the consequences of the common notions all the way down into the space of everyday ethical decision making. Spinoza thinks that the ethicist can have the same epistemic certainty about ethical problems that the geometer has about geometric ones. But the common notions, which serve as regulatory rules for rational thinking, are themselves abstract principles that we do not necessarily apply to our lived experience. Knowing by the second kind of knowledge entails knowing the axiom that governs clear and distinct thoughts, but it does not involve developing clear and distinct thoughts about singular things, only about the abstract rules of thinking that govern how later one can properly grasp the essence of a singular thing.

So, Spinoza asserts that the common notions *qua* metaphysical are the axioms that govern metaphysical thought. But law of the universe dictates that there must be axioms to govern metaphysics in the first place? Most simply put, a mind that relates all sensory input to a collection of rational principles is a rational one, and that set of rational principles itself constitutes reason. The grasping of common notions consists in the uncovering of the principles that govern the natural world insofar as it is metaphysical. All extended bodies—all material things—agree in that they have properties reflective of these metaphysical principles. For Spinoza, these axioms as we represent them are not necessarily inherent in nature but are rather necessary according to the human mind (IIP38C) and the way the mind systematically constructs frameworks for thinking. However, that which the axiomatic representation of the common notion reflects is precisely what the human body as a part of nature shares with the material things outside the human body. The human being only grasps a principle about efficient causality because it is efficiently caused. Both the human body and the material world outside of the human body adhere to the same set of abstract principles, but the way the human mind represents them—i.e., propositionally and metaphysically—is decisively human.

Although Spinoza thinks that the propositional mode of representing common notions is a human artifact, most interpreters read Spinoza as believing that the human mind, which has access to the metaphysical

laws of nature through propositional knowledge, actually
has a quasi-mystical idea of some divine property of the
thing itself. This means that, when one takes the
proposition away, left in the mind is some bare
metaphysical truth. But it is hard to see how an idea could
harbor any content without the human element of
language. And the language itself cannot constitute the
idea, but only points to it. So, I would temper this robust
claim by asserting that the metaphysical axioms he applies
in the *Ethics* are powerful enough as principles that govern
rational thought but need not be seen as mystical
windows into the heart of the universe's divine essence.
Still, the remarkable problem concerning scientific
thought is not just that it works well, but why it does.

Now that I have summarized Spinoza's view, I
shall now attempt to retrieve some of Spinoza's thoughts
about rational principles in a more appealing light. I shall
do this by applying Wilfrid Sellars's famous concept of
the 'myth of the given' to the Spinozist conception of
common notions. Sellars defines the Myth as follows:

> *The idea* that observation "strictly and properly
> so-called" is constituted by certain self-
> authenticating nonverbal episodes, the authority
> of which is translated to verbal and quasi-verbal
> performances when these performances are
> made "in conformity with the semantical rules of
> the language," is, of course, the heart of the Myth
> of the Given.

Sellars's notion of the myth of the given attacks both
rationalist and empiricist epistemology. In light of
Spinozist common notions, Sellars might raise the
objection that the principles of reason according to which
a person gains true knowledge themselves depend on
conceptual experiences that impress upon the mind the
nature of those very principles. For Sellars, there is no

pre-existing rational structure to reality or to the human mind. There is no property of the human mind 'beneath' the axiom—the axiom itself is the property that the mind has learned and conceptualized. But Spinoza seems to treat his axioms as artifacts of the mental that give us unmediated access to the true laws of nature. The Sellarsian critique allows us to force open the possibility of modifying the axiomatic principles that govern rational thought about empirical science, or at least of seeing it in a different light. What I intend to convey by citing Sellars is that the philosopher can healthily reduce the metaphysical principles that Spinoza interprets as indicative of 'things in themselves' to linguistic technologies that open up new modes of thinking and seeing. The truth of the axioms must be a truth that one self-consciously holds true in light of the meaning of the concepts and their utility, not because they reflect or are some inherent property of the divine essence. One can find a forceful critique of the rationalist foundationalist picture—that all human knowledge rests on self-evident givens like the *cogito*—in the work of Michel Foucault, who analyzes the social institutions and practices that govern the rational precepts that produce pieces of knowledge.

Spinoza's development of Cartesian common notions provides the possibility of setting up the psychological rules that necessitate clear and distinct thought. But, yet to be applied to individual things, Spinoza's common notions exist as mere abstractions, as guidelines that determine the bounds of sense according to which one can have knowledge. However, Sellars warns readers of Spinoza (indirectly) to check the temptation to project propositional knowledge onto the nature as though the contents of the rational axioms were the essential properties of a human mind that has a connatural channel to the divinity that shapes our ends. My solution to the problem of how to temper Spinoza's forceful claim, not the first of its kind, is to view the guidelines for propositional thought as linguistic technologies. Were he alive today, Spinoza may not ultimately be too opposed to this. But, influenced by the Cartesian worries about Neo-Pyrrhonists like Montaigne, Spinoza ultimately adopted view that the mind can develop unmediated access to the very ideas that comprise the laws of nature. Today, one might read Spinoza's epistemology in a mitigated way, that incorporates his rational principles as artifacts of reason, as tools that one can either take up or dispose of and that govern certain areas of human knowledge instead of as a foundation of all knowledge. The reason for this is that Spinoza's emphasis on common notions represents a limited perspective on what constitutes intelligence.

THE THIRD KIND OF KNOWLEDGE

W e now have the tools to get to the heart of Spinoza's science. The title of this book refers to the name for the third kind of knowledge that Spinoza offers us: *scientia intuitiva*, or intuitive science. He defines intuitive science as knowledge that proceeds from the common notions—scientific principles founded on the study of the natural world—to the grasping of the essences of the particular things that we encounter in sensory experience. The third kind of knowledge, for Spinoza, pertains to mental states that I think of as an alloy of kinds one and two. Instead of being restricted purely to extension, purely to thought, the mind in the third kind of knowledge sees to its thinking in the immanent plane of actual being. If the reader has covered the text with scrupulous care so far, the gist of the third kind of knowledge will be clear. But in order to explicate the concept in full, so as not to present an unintelligible mess to the reader, I must retrace several basic concepts in Spinoza's thought as a sort of pedagogical interlude.

I have only hinted in places at Spinoza's metaphysical ontology. Here, I shall briefly summarize his account of substance, the attributes of substance, and the modifications of substance, because these notions come into play more heavily within discourse about the third kind of knowledge. First, substance: Spinoza imagines himself as having parted ways with his Cartesian and Aristotelian predecessors by positing that there is ultimately only one kind of thing that actually exists. All the things that the human mind separates in thought are part of the same substance. This substance is the common, immanent plane of being on which everything that is, is. This substance goes by various names, such as Nature, God, and Being. Spinoza's innovation here is not so much his ascription of the term substance to nature as a whole, but his refusal to use the word '*substantia*' in any sense but to refer to the common, immanent plane of being. One way of thinking about substance is that it is the container—mental and physical—in which everything that exists occurs. For many others, this thought about nature as a whole consisted in *primary* substance, which implies an infinite number of secondary substances. Spinoza, however, restricted the word to signify nature taken as the whole, the 'in-which' of all thought and all matter.

Now, I speak of thought and matter. Following Descartes, Spinoza believed that this substance, though unary, has two attributes that the human mind can grasp. These two attributes are thought (*cogitatio*) and extension (*extensio*). Though substance necessarily has infinite attributes, the human mind can regard substance under these two aspects. On the one hand, I can experience the plane of being according to how my sense organs relate to my extended environment. On the other hand, I can cogitate on the scientific principles that, for Spinoza, consist in the 'why' of the laws of the universe. The distinction involves the human mind's regarding substance at one time as extension, at the other as thought, but substance as such always remains in a state of unity.

I mentioned earlier that substance is the container, the 'in-which' in which all singular things take place. This in-which is both mental and physical, and Spinoza thinks of the mental and physical as explicitly parallel to one another, a doctrine called parallelism. But he still wants to divide up the things that happen within nature, and the name for a singular thing that happen on the immanent plane of the natural is 'mode'. The mode or modification of the natural pertains to objects that nature both conceives according to its scientific properties and laws and that nature expresses as part of the extended world. All things in human experience are these modifications of substance, and they are of substance in the sense that they occur within the immanent plane of the natural, a conception of nature which holds parallel to one another both psychological and physical properties of each singular thing.

But what does all this metaphysical jargon mean for us? Well, Spinoza thinks that each human being is a mode through which nature expresses itself. And the human body is both an extended thing and a thing that accesses the ideas that comprise the mental essence of nature. Many philosophers scoff at the idea of things like rocks as having 'minds', and I think Spinoza would too, though some philosophers are willing to assert that this is Spinoza's view. But what he seems to mean is that objects like stones participate in the same aspect of nature, thought, by which human beings psychologically access the natural world. We can grasp the 'ideas' that a stone 'has' by interrogating it according to analytic or synthetic theorizing. But this doesn't mean that the stone 'thinks' like a human being does. Nor does it mean that the human body is subject to principles of physics much different than that to which a stone is subject.

Let's now turn to the third kind of knowledge. Now, we know the human mind can access the singular things that occur in nature under two different modes of inquiry; I can see, e.g., a pen as a physical object obedient of the laws of physics but as an extended entity in the realm of actual existence, and I can interrogate that same object according only to those laws. This is where the two prior kinds of knowledge come in: the first kind of knowledge is the kind of perceptual activity in which I take the extended world as the ultimate reality. The second kind of knowledge sets aside the extended world and interrogates the nature according to the laws that govern it. Finally, the third kind of knowledge is the highest possibility for the human being, the human mode of substance, because it consists in the unified experience of the thing both according to extension and to thought. Not only do I have a principled grasp of why things are the way they are, but I bring that understanding to bear on things that I actually encounter in my lived experience.

Spinoza, at first glance, seems like the kind of philosopher who thinks that the virtuous ought to coup up in her study and develop scientific principles. But without bringing that knowledge to bear on reality, without seeing to that knowledge in an execution of it, the human being lives a lopsided existence that engages with nature only in one of its aspects. The third kind of knowledge is the mind's highest virtue, because it involves the human modification's purest actualization of the divinity within the human creature—the full power of thought and extension as one.

The analytic method, as I said above, entails a meditative thought process that elicits axiomatic principles from the meditator. Spinoza as a meditator himself then elected to arrange those definitions and axioms into the framework of ethics by means of synthesis, which would allow him to demonstrate logically the truth of his conclusions. The work, of course, has its force when one has arrived at the identical truths according to their own meditation. Consider the following diagrams that I've designed to make this explicitly clear.

Once meditators reach those principles through a metaphysical analysis of their various ideas, they are ready to confront physical objects according to those axioms (the common notions). See Diagram 1. This ensures that rational principles rather than random perceptions and emotions direct our interaction with the objects of sensation. In short, the act of the mind that consists in the third kind of knowledge involves the grasping of the essence of an extended thing in a single glance. See Diagram 2. The potential to know in this way becomes accessible to the human being according to first, the development of a view of the rational principles that ought to govern perceptual thought and second, the rationalized experience of singular things that allows us to see them in a clear and distinct way.

Some interpreters have lamented that Spinoza depicts only mathematical examples of the third kind of knowledge that cannot possibly problematize his epistemic views. At IIP40S2, he thinks about the third kind of knowledge in terms of a grasp of mathematical properties that allow the human mind to solve an equation instantaneously. But we have seen that Spinoza follows Descartes in his belief that axiomatic principles not only govern mathematical and logical thinking, but also metaphysical reality. For Spinoza, adequate definitions of various social, political, or psychological categories in conjunction with axiomatic grounds don't just increase the likelihood but necessitate that what a person says or thinks about some singular thing is true. Spinoza's science need not be restricted to mathematical entities but can be applied to any field in which there are definitions and axioms in place. This is why he calls his work the *Ethics Demonstrated in Geometric Order*—he intends to set forth metaphysical axioms and definitions that prove incontrovertibly the ethical propositions that follow.

Until now, I have given little content to Spinoza's method of ethical science. Having treated his epistemological thought in this way, I have omitted the ethical upshot of Spinoza's claims; essentially, Spinoza desires to offer the invitation to discover an objective, parent framework that the human being can always apply in relation to the singular objects it experiences. Aristotle would generally argue that the world of entities that do not exist within abstract, axiomatized systems like mathematics or logic simply cannot be theorized in the same way. As I said before, it is here that Spinoza offers a radical reinterpretation of human possibility: namely, by using demonstration as his method, he necessarily sets out to *prove* both that there is always a right answer even to complex ethical problems and to offer a picture of what that answer looks like.

SPINOZA'S SCIENCE

Before I turn to my final arguments, I'd like to summarize what has been said before by acknowledging Spinoza's trifold distinction between kinds of knowledge in the diagram below. In particular, I would like to pose two questions that can be put as follows: 1) What kind of datum does each kind of knowledge have as its object? 2) As what does the interpreter take the experience of that datum? In other words, what is the story the knower tells himself about the true nature of the thing as it relates to the data it has? The following table summarizes the three kinds alongside the data of each kind and what the interpreter takes the datum to be. By 'taken as', I mean nothing but the extent to which the interpreter endorses the proposition that the perceived entity is in itself so.

Summary of Spinoza's Three Kinds of Knowledge		
Kind	*Object*	*Taken As*
Opinion or Imagination (First)	Sense-impressions and emotions.	The thing's essence.
Reason (Second)	Common notions.	Universal Laws
Intuitive Science (Third)	The things essence.	The thing's essence.

In this chapter, I concern myself with how one might apply Spinoza's third kind of knowledge. I have shown above that the third kind of knowledge, intuitive science, pertains to psychological experiences which involve a triangulation of common notions around an object given in sensory or imaginative experience. The mind uses and applies the metaphysical and scientific principles on which it has a firm hold by letting the singular thing insert itself into the function of the relevant common notions. In Spinoza's view, the subject of intuitive science executes this process so as to form the idea of the thing itself. The common notions fall by the wayside but serve as constraints upon veridical thought. These constraints leave the mind with a pure experience of the object. Intuitive science of a singular thing is knowledge of that thing's essence.

In this final chapter, I am focused on extracting the basic implications of that account of third kind of knowledge—what I call **Spinoza's Science**—and then employing that understanding for the purpose of making clear the most serious possible ethical statement I can muster on the basis of what Spinoza has made available. I'm more bashful than to claim the universality of my perspective, but hopefully the readers, whoever you are, will find a way to make use of how I think Spinoza's statements can be best applied. Indeed, it is in the space of dealing with emotions and in the transmutation of suffering from dreadful to empowering that Spinoza shines most brilliantly with respect to his contemporaries.

Again, the third kind of knowledge involves intellectual acts wherein the mind both 1) has a grasp of the axiomatic bounds of rational thinking and 2) experiences a psychological image (a sensation or a memory) that the mind contemplates according to those axiomatic boundaries. In this way, the human being expresses the entirety of its power, for it embodies in full potency both thought and extension. The mind not only thinks on the basis of rational principles, but experiences objects according to them.

Spinoza is not the only philosopher who thinks that people's beliefs about the world inform our perceptual content of it. In early childhood, the mind begins forming a metaphysical understanding of the world. It places things into certain categories of existence according to what it experiences. Spinoza wants to break philosophers free of the continuum that keeps them dependent on positive experiences in order to feel good about themselves. Random events can certainly help, but they can also harm. *Axiomatic understanding of metaphysical reality empowers the mind to transmute what may have been an episode of anguish into positive meaning.*

The possessor of the third kind of knowledge has already arrived at the axiomatic principles of reason by way of the analytic method. The ethical way of life then is already set in motion. Disposed to act rationally, the virtuous simply lives as they have before, but this time equipped with principles of reason by which they can see the things in the world in their essential nature. I shall refer to this disposition toward perceptual reality—being in possession of rational axioms—as a virtuous disposition.

Now that the reader has a picture of the virtuous disposition, which simply consists in a name for the state of an individual who possesses the truths about how to think about any kind of event in an empowering way, the question becomes, what does this virtuous disposition look like when it is applied? The question can be as complex and difficult as we'd like it to be. Many philosophers have criticized Spinoza for having oversimplified the task of cultivating the virtuous disposition by explaining it by means of examples from elementary mathematics, a conceptual region that operates according to an explicable set of rules and practices that tell the operator what to do in every circumstance. But what about more challenging, more complex ethical situations, where the rules by which one should operate are not so obvious? Spinoza knows that he is in no position to make such decisions for those who study his work. Like his philosophical forbears, most famously Socrates, he would rather place students in a position to make the correct ethical decision on their own.

He offers us the possibility of becoming ethical agents *through* a form of rationalist self-cultivation.

Human beings who live according to the first kind of knowledge allow random experience to govern the perceptual phenomena that arise in their intellects. This means that people's sensations and emotions—together, their perceptions—reflect how they interpret that their day or life is going. Mirroring is important in child psychology, because the child can only grasp its own safety and sense of importance through the way the world treats it. But a major premise of 'being-an-adult' is that adults develop the ability to derive their own self-respect from their own inward reflection. And binding one's self-regard to how one is randomly treated makes a person inconstant and incontinent. Canto 5 in Dante's *Inferno* wonderfully describes the incontinent as so *light* that they are battered up, down, left, and right—whatever direction the wind blows. For Spinoza, when experiences dictate the entirety of what human beings feel, this means that subjects, though capable, play only a passive role in their own lives. They have little or no awareness of themselves as psychic agents because their haphazard experiences are impressing perceptions so powerful that they dominate their psyche. The sway of powerful emotions alienates epistemic and ethical subjects from the possibility that they ever play an active role in their own lives. The Latin word for 'weight' is *pondus*, from which English takes its word 'ponderous'. The Western philosophical tradition that begins with Socrates has called the flighty, inconstant, and light subject to recognize itself as the subject of its own actions. This self-recognition opens the subject to the possibility of standing its ground against conspicuously harmful perceptions, emotions, and desires.

Spinoza's call to ethical agency, then, involves taking a modified Socratic perspective on emotions and experiences. He calls one into ethical maturity and agency.

This maturity necessarily involves knowing one's own human body—one's own memories, experiences, beliefs, and dispositions—because each human body contains the signature of a series of life experiences that have determined that disposition to perceptual experience. Rational actors can see the emotion that wants to impinge on clear and distinct perception *as* an impinging emotion, one that tells them little or nothing about the local situation that seem to have caused the feeling, one that is perhaps bound up in a habitual way of thinking distortedly. For Spinoza, a perceptual experience that an excessive or deficient emotional response mediates becomes clouded by one's personal history of way of thinking. Spinoza thought it both desirable and possible that the mind could elaborate such a principled way of life that it could uncouple certain 'negative' emotions like sadness, anger, and fear from the sensations and interpretations of the situations it perceives.

I should like to close with a metaphor—the symbol of *smoke*—to explain how Spinoza wants to adjust the human mind's relationship to its own emotions. Now, I can interpret smoke as a symbol in many ways, but I should like to focus on two of them. (1) Smoke can be that which stands between my sight and the object that I am trying to see. This is how the emotions function. But (2) the symbol smoke also calls to mind its use as a signal. This presents the active intellect with a twofold task. The first is to understand that the world will objectify the mind until I definitively become an active agent in my own perceptual being: until I see emotions as emotions, until I see that something is in the way, that emotions and sensations are imposing themselves onto my ability to perceive clearly, I shall never understand what I am looking at. The moment that I think of the emotions *as* emotions in place of thinking of the emotions as bound up with my experiences, and of sensations *as* sensations, I achieve the joy of intellectual understanding. Rather than think of this same smoke as that which obfuscates my view of perceptual reality, I now think of it as a signal, cue, or clue. I am in some way called to understand its causes and its meaning, and, on the Spinozist view, once I do, I shall finally be able to clarify what I am actually trying to see. This is a profoundly difficult task, not because the concept of truth is intellectually difficult to grasp, but because the capacity to project specters of the past onto people, places, and things often fools people into thinking that they are seeing truth; but they are more seriously in a dialogue with the phantasmata of a jumble between their sensations and emotions. Spinoza labors, as well as he can, to depict discursively the step by step path that any person—anyone who is willing to undertake the daunting task of thinking of projection as projection, emotion as emotion—must take in order to become truly wise and truly blessed.

CONCLUSION

This account of Spinoza's science can be closed by pointing to two major challenges that confront one's ability simply to appropriate the Spinozist view wholesale. Although Spinoza thought radically insofar as he subordinated Judeo-Christian ethical teachings to logic and rationalism, he still appears to have believed in a form of ultimate reality, a nature that is governed by the rational principles that apply everywhere and anywhere. Many philosophers who work in epistemology today do not adhere to the same theological assumptions that undergird Spinoza's work. These assumptions about the nature of an 'ultimate reality' converge in both Spinozist epistemology and ethics. Spinoza did not foresee numerous challenges that would arise from philosophy's newfound capacity call into question the foundationalist assumptions of religious dogma—namely, the belief in a certain perspective of God as such—despite that he, Descartes, and others provided the instruments by which later philosophers would confront those assumptions. The work of Friedrich Nietzsche, for example, did not merely consist in the Spinozist critique that religious teachings required proof like any other thesis, but advanced it another step by questioning whether ethical teachings were inherently justified in calling themselves 'good', 'righteous', and 'just'. Nietzsche looked at the work of Copernicus, Darwin, and Descartes and came to question what were the psychological mechanics by which a person came flatly to assume that their own actions were 'good' and another's 'evil'.

Spinoza stood even further from having foreseen the 20th century critiques of Cartesian science that philosophers like Wilfrid Sellars and especially Martin Heidegger mounted in order to call into question certain pieties of science, the view that scientific thinking as a mode of inquiry uncovers the given nature of some ultimate reality. These revolutions—both in the fields of epistemology and ethics—radically call into question the notion that Spinoza's picture, even of the third kind of knowledge, the highest form of human existence, ought ever to satisfy a person who is truly hungry for knowledge and ethical growth. Spinoza alludes to his own doubts but not forcefully. Many have come to see bits of knowledge as internal to the assumptions that govern them. Spinoza can well name a certain range of perceptual experience 'good' and then aim to fall within that range, but what criteria determine that those perceptual and emotional experiences be good and others not?

However, the social norms that govern modern culture—to oversimplify grossly—have in many ways hardly changed despite major upheavals in the ways that these norms are enforced. Philosophers like Michel Foucault, Elizabeth Anscombe, G.E. Moore, and countless others have pointed out that the dominant culture no longer accepts religious dogmata as premises sufficient to direct ethical behavior, and yet that same culture still oftentimes severely enforces social norms and standards remarkably similar to those that were developed according to assumptions the nobody any longer believes in. Why is this so? How does this complicate the possibility of any grand project of ethics?

Spinoza himself recognized that ethical problems often have no straightforward and easy solutions. The truth is not transparently or inherently accessible to the untutored mind—it requires a rigorous and directed effort, one that balances the ways in which emotions can influence belief and the ways in which sensations that only reflect the way an object *appears to the mind* can guide the intellect into habitual states of misperception that take appearance as reality. While he may have been overly willing to attempt to formulate a set of universal precepts that could govern all human decisions, his philosophy at least captures the core difficulties—distinguishing between feelings and appearances, appearances and reality—that come in the way of getting things right.

DIAGRAMS

1. *Cartesian Meditative Analysis*

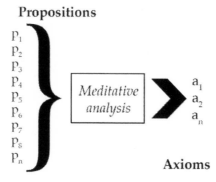

Figure 1. The meditator takes a vast array of propositions about the world (p1...pn) in meditative analysis and distills them into axioms (a1...an).

2. *The Third Kind of Knowledge*

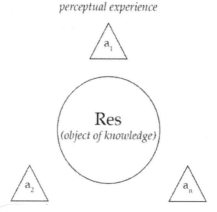

Figure 2. Third kind of knowledge. The truths arrived at in the meditation then come to direct the meditator's thinking about the thing it experiences.

WORKS CITED

Bennett, Jonathan. *A Study of Spinozas Ethics*. Indianapolis, IN: Hackett Publishing, 1984.

Curley, Edwin M. *Spinoza: Issues and Directions: The Proceedings of the Chicago Spinoza Conference*. Leiden: Brill, 1990.

De Spinoza, Benedictus. *Ethica Ordine Geometrico Demonstrata*. San Bernardino, CA: Perfect Library, 2015.

Deleuze, Gilles, and Robert Hurley. *Spinoza: Practical Philosophy*. San Francisco: City Lights Books, 1988.

Deleuze, Gilles, and Martin Joughin. *Expressionism in Philosophy Spinoza*. New York: Zone Books, 2013.

Descartes, René. *Selected Philosophical Writings*. Translated by John Cottingham, Robert Stoothoff, and Dugald Murdoch. New York, NY: Cambridge University Press, 1998.

Fløistad, Guttorm. "Spinozas Theory of Knowledge." *Inquiry* 12, no. 1-4 (1969): 41-65. doi:10.1080/00201746908601550.

Garrett, Aaron V. *Meaning in Spinoza's Method*. Cambridge, UK: Cambridge University Press, 2003.

Grene, Marjorie. *Spinoza: A Collection of Critical Essays*. Univ. of Notre Dame Press, 1984.

Lord, Beth. *Spinozas Ethics: An Edinburgh Philosophical Guide (Edinburgh Philosophical Guides Series)*. Edinburgh University Press, 2010.

Nadler, Steven M. *Spionozas Ethics: An Introduction*. New York: Cambridge University Press, 2009.

Spinoza, Benedictus De, E. M. Curley, and Stuart Hampshire. *Ethics*. London: Penguin Books, 2005.

Made in the USA
San Bernardino, CA
06 May 2020